SO-ACS-548

technology of the
modern world

technology of the
modern world

Edited by Zoe Lowery

Britannica®
Educational Publishing

IN ASSOCIATION WITH

ROSEN
EDUCATIONAL SERVICES

Published in 2016 by Britannica Educational Publishing (a trademark of Encyclopædia Britannica, Inc.) in association with The Rosen Publishing Group, Inc.
29 East 21st Street, New York, NY 10010

To see additional Britannica Educational Publishing titles, go to rosenpublishing.com.
First Edition

Britannica Educational Publishing
J.E. Luebering: Director, Core Reference Group
Anthony L. Green: Editor, Compton's by Britannica

Rosen Publishing
Zoe Lowery: Editor
Nelson Sá: Art Director
Nicole Russo: Designer
Cindy Reiman: Photography Manager
Bruce Donnola: Photo Researcher
Introduction and supplementary material by Jason Porterfield.

Cataloging-in-Publication Data
Technology of the modern world / edited by Zoe Lowery. — First edition.
    pages cm. — (The history of technology)
 Includes bibliographical references and index.
 ISBN 978-1-68048-276-8 (library bound)
 1. Technology—History—20th century—Juvenile literature. 2. Technological innovations—History—20th century—Juvenile literature. I. Lowery, Zoe, editor.
 T48.T45 2016
 609.04—dc23

Manufactured in the United States of America

Contents

Introduction

The rapid pace of technological change in the 20th century makes it difficult to put these recent developments in historical perspective. New materials, ranging from synthetic rubber to plastics and artificial fabrics, affected ways of life and fashion. With the introduction of the electric streetcar in 1888, cities extended beyond the distance that could easily be covered by a horse. Following the establishment of the assembly line by Henry Ford in 1913, the automobile became inexpensive enough for many to afford one and changed the landscape in industrialized nations. The aircraft industry grew within decades after the first powered flight by the Wright brothers in 1903.

The age of electronics was ushered in when Marconi sent the first transatlantic radio message in 1901. Radio and, later, television changed communications and entertainment habits.

Although early computing machines existed by World War II, it took the invention of the transistor in 1948 to make modern computers and office machines a reality. Nuclear power was introduced after World War II, and the space age began with the first Soviet spacecraft in 1957. Many of these developments depended on the advances in science that were required before their adaptation by engineers.

As technology advances, it allows further exploration of space. NASA's Curiosity rover explored Mars from 2012 and took this "selfie" in 2014.

Medical technology, which started with better sanitary practices in the 19th century, was expanded by the use of new medicines and new equipment. These developments nearly doubled the life span of a person living in an industrialized country compared to 100 years earlier. New technologies in biology led to genetic engineering, in which living cells can be altered.

In weaponry there was the invention of the tank, the perfection of the airplane, and, finally, the use of the atomic bomb. These changed warfare from what had been primarily an encounter between military personnel to putting all peoples of the world at risk.

Technology keeps advancing at a rapid rate. It can only be guessed what will follow the "information revolution" that began in the late 20th century.

Communications took a major step forward with the development of the Internet in the 1970s. Powerful microchips led to smaller and more affordable computers. The invention of the World Wide Web in 1989 and its introduction to the world at large in 1991 represented a major shift in how information was exchanged.

For the next quarter century, communications continued to evolve. Faster, smaller, and more powerful computer processors led to the introduction of portable devices such as smart-phones and wearable technology. Wireless networks made these advances possible.

Rising fossil fuel prices and concerns about global warming in the first decade of the 21st century led to an increased interest in developing renewable fuel sources. Steps were taken to modernize power grids and increase fuel efficiency. Solar and wind energy became more significant contributors to the power supply as companies invested in improving existing technology. Electric cars and hybrid vehicles became a reality after years of development.

Human ingenuity continues to drive new innovations and the development of even more advanced technology as people strive to find new ways to solve problems or make life easier. "First, be sure a thing is wanted or needed, then go ahead," the great inventor Thomas Edison once advised. *Technology of the Modern World* offers a brief, but insightful glance at some of the most remarkable advances of the last century.

TECHNOLOGY FROM 1900 TO 1945

R ecent history is notoriously difficult to write because of the mass of material and the problem of distinguishing the significant from the insignificant among events that have virtually the power of contemporary experience. In respect to the recent history of technology, however, one fact stands out clearly: Despite the immense achievements of technology by 1900, the following decades witnessed more advance over a wide range of activities than the whole of previously recorded history. The airplane, the rocket and interplanetary probes, electronics, atomic power, antibiotics, insecticides, and a host of new materials have all been invented and developed to create an unparalleled social situation, full of possibilities and dangers, which would have been virtually unimaginable before the 20th century.

In venturing to interpret the events of the previous century, it will be convenient to separate the years before 1945 from those that followed. The years 1900 to 1945 were dominated by the two world wars, while those since 1945 were preoccupied by the need to avoid another major war. The dividing point is one of outstanding social and technological significance: the detonation of the first atomic bomb at Alamogordo, N.M., in July 1945.

There were profound political changes in the 20th century related to technological capacity and leadership. It may be an exaggeration to regard the 20th century as "the American century," but the rise of the United States as a superstate was sufficiently rapid and dramatic to excuse the hyperbole. It was a rise based upon tremendous natural resources exploited to secure increased productivity through widespread industrialization, and the success of the United States in achieving this objective was tested and demonstrated in the two world wars. Technological leadership passed from Britain and the European nations to the United States in the course of these wars. This is not to say that the springs of innovation went dry in Europe. Many important inventions of the 20th century originated there. But it was the United States that had the capacity to assimilate innovations and take full advantage from them at times when other countries were deficient in one or other of the vital social resources without which a brilliant invention cannot be converted into a commercial success. As with Britain in the Industrial Revolution, the technological vitality of the United States in the 20th century was demonstrated less by any particular innovations than by its ability to adopt new ideas from whatever source they came.

The two world wars were themselves the most important instruments of technological as well as political change in the 20th century. The rapid evolution of the airplane is a striking illustration of this process, while the appearance of the tank in the first conflict and of the atomic bomb in the second show the same signs of response to an urgent military stimulus. It has been said that World War I was a chemists' war, on the basis of the immense importance of high explosives and poison gas. In other respects the two wars hastened the development of technology by extending the institutional apparatus for the encouragement of innovation by both the state and private industry. This process went further in some countries than in others, but no major belligerent nation could resist entirely the need to support and coordinate its scientific-technological effort. The wars were thus responsible for speeding the transformation from "little science," with research still largely restricted to small-scale efforts by a few isolated scientists, to "big science," with the emphasis on large research teams sponsored by governments and corporations, working collectively on the development and application of new techniques. While the extent of this transformation must not be overstated, and recent research has tended to stress the continuing need for the independent inventor at least in the stimulation of innovation, there can be little doubt that the change in the scale of technological enterprises had far-reaching consequences. It was one of the most momentous transformations of the 20th century, for it altered the quality of industrial and social organization. In the process it assured technology, for the first time in its long history, a position of importance and even honor in social esteem.

FUEL AND POWER

There were no fundamental innovations in fuel and power before the breakthrough of 1945, but there were several significant developments in techniques that had originated in the previous century. An outstanding development of this type was the internal-combustion

German engineer Rudolf Diesel invented the diesel engine in the 1890s. The speed and efficiency of modern travel by ship and railroad train is due in large part to this invention.

engine, which was continuously improved to meet the needs of road vehicles and airplanes. The high-compression engine burning heavy-oil fuels, invented by Rudolf Diesel in the 1890s, was developed to serve as a submarine power unit in World War I and was subsequently adapted to heavy road haulage duties and to agricultural tractors. Moreover, the sort of development that had transformed the reciprocating steam engine into the steam turbine occurred with the internal-combustion engine, the gas turbine replacing the reciprocating engine for specialized purposes such as aero-engines, in which a high power-to-weight ratio is important. Admittedly, this adaptation had not proceeded very far by 1945, although the first jet-powered aircraft were in service by the end of the war. The theory of the gas turbine, however, had been understood since the 1920s at least, and in 1929 Sir Frank Whittle, then taking a flying instructor's course with the Royal Air Force, combined it with the principle of jet propulsion in the engine for which he took out a patent in the following year. But the construction of a satisfactory gas-turbine engine was delayed for a decade by the lack of resources, and particularly by the need to develop new metal alloys that could withstand the high temperatures generated in the engine. This problem was solved by the development of a nickel-chromium alloy, and, with the gradual solution of the other problems, work went on in both Germany and Britain to seize a military advantage by applying the jet engine to combat aircraft.

Until 1945, electricity and the internal-combustion engine were the dominant sources of power for industry and transport in the 20th century, although in some parts of the industrialized world steam power and even older prime movers remained important. Early research in nuclear physics was more scientific than technological, stirring little general interest. In fact, from the work of Ernest Rutherford, Albert Einstein, and others to the first successful experiments in splitting heavy atoms in Germany in 1938, no particular thought was given to engineering potential. The war led the Manhattan Project to produce the fission bomb that was first exploded at Alamogordo, N.M. Only in its final stages did even this program become a matter of technology, when the problems of building large reactors and handling radioactive materials had to be solved. At this point it also became an economic and political matter, because very heavy capital expenditure was involved. Thus, in this crucial event of the mid-20th century, the convergence of science, technology, economics, and politics finally took place.

INDUSTRY AND INNOVATION

There were technological innovations of great significance in many aspects of industrial production during the 20th century. It is worth observing, in the first place, that the basic matter of industrial organization became one of self-conscious innovation, with organizations setting out to increase their productivity by improved techniques. Methods of work study, first systematically examined in the United States at the end of the 19th century, were widely applied in U.S. and European industrial organizations in the first half of the 20th century, evolving rapidly into scientific management and the modern studies of industrial administration, organization and method, and particular managerial techniques. The object of these exercises was to make industry more efficient and thus to increase productivity and profits, and there can be no doubt that they were remarkably successful, if not quite as successful as some of their advocates maintained. Without this superior industrial organization, it would not have been possible to convert the comparatively small workshops of the 19th century into the giant engineering establishments of the 20th, with their mass-production and assembly-line techniques. The rationalization of production, so characteristic of industry in the 20th century, may thus be legitimately regarded as the result of the application of new techniques that form part of the history of technology since 1900.

Among multiple fields of industrial innovation in the 20th century was the production of new materials. As far as volume of consumption goes, humankind still lives in the Iron Age, with the utilization of iron exceeding that of any other material. In the 20th century steel alloys multiplied.

FOOD AND AGRICULTURE

The increasing chemical understanding of drugs and microorganisms was applied with outstanding success to the study of food. The analysis of the relationship between certain types of food and human physical performance led to the identification of vitamins in 1911 and to their classification into three types in 1919, with subsequent additions and subdivisions. It was realized that the presence of these materials is necessary for a healthy diet, and eating habits and public health programs were adjusted accordingly. The importance of trace elements, very minor constituents, was also discovered and investigated, beginning in

1895 with the realization that a goitre could be caused by a deficiency of iodine.

As well as improving in quality, the quantity of food produced in the 20th century increased rapidly as a result of the intensive application of modern technology. The greater scale and complexity of urban life created a pressure for increased production and a greater variety of foodstuffs, and the resources of the internal-combustion engine, electricity, and chemical technology were called upon to achieve these objectives. The internal-combustion engine was utilized in the tractor, which became the almost universal agent of mobile power on the farm in the industrialized countries. The same engines powered other machines such as combine harvesters, which became common in the United States in the early 20th century, although their use was less widespread in the more labour-intensive farms of Europe, especially before World War II. Synthetic fertilizers, an important product of the chemical industry, became popular in most types of farming, and other chemicals—pesticides and herbicides—appeared toward the end of the period, effecting something of an agrarian revolution. Once again, World War II gave a powerful boost to development. Despite problems of pollution that developed later, the introduction of DDT as a highly effective insecticide in 1944 was a particularly significant achievement of chemical technology. Food processing and packaging also advanced—dehydration techniques such as

Canning vegetables and other foods remains a popular technique for preserving, although in the 20th century vacuum drying and other dehydration techniques were introduced.

vacuum-contact drying were introduced in the 1930s—but the 19th-century innovations of canning and refrigeration remained the dominant techniques of preservation.

CIVIL ENGINEERING

Important development occurred in civil engineering in the first half of the 20th century, although there were few striking innovations. Advancing techniques for large-scale construction produced many spectacular skyscrapers, bridges, and dams all over the world but especially in the United States. New York City acquired its characteristic skyline, built upon the exploitation of steel frames and reinforced concrete. Conventional methods of building in brick and masonry had reached the limits of feasibility in the 1800s in office blocks up to 16-stories high, and the future lay with the skeleton frame or cage construction pioneered in the 1880s in Chicago. The vital ingredients for the new tall buildings or

THE TRACTOR

The first applications to agriculture of the four-stroke-cycle gasoline engine were as stationary engines, at first in Germany, later elsewhere. By the 1890s stationary engines were mounted on wheels to make them portable, and soon a drive was added to make them self-propelled. The first successful gasoline tractor was built in the United States in 1892. Soon several companies were manufacturing tractors worldwide. The number of tractors in the more developed countries increased dramatically during the 20th century, especially in the United States: In 1907 some 600 tractors were in use, but the figure had grown to almost 3,400,000 by 1950.

Improvements such as the diesel engine and four-wheel drive made for faster tractors with the power to pull heavier loads.

Twentieth-century changes in tractor design produced a more efficient and useful machine. Principal among these were the power takeoff, introduced in 1918, in which power from the tractor's engine could be transmitted directly to an implement through the use of a special shaft; the all-purpose, or tricycle-type, tractor (1924), which enabled farmers to cultivate planted crops mechanically; rubber tires (1932), which facilitated faster operating speeds; and the switch to four-wheel drives and diesel power in the 1950s and 1960s, which greatly increased the tractor's pulling power. The last innovations have led to the development of enormous tractors—usually having double tires on each wheel and enclosed, air-conditioned cabs—that can pull several gangs of plows.

skyscrapers that followed were abundant cheap steel—for columns, beams, and trusses—and efficient passenger elevators. The availability of these developments and the demand for more and more office space in the thriving cities of Chicago and New York caused the boom in skyscraper building that continued until 1931, when the Empire State Building, with its total height of 1,250 feet (381 metres) and 102 stories, achieved a limit not exceeded for 40 years and demonstrated the strength of its structure by sustaining the crash impact of a B-25 bomber in July 1945 with only minor damage to the building. The Great Depression brought a halt to skyscraper building from 1932 until after World War II.

Concrete, and more especially reinforced concrete (that is, concrete set around a framework or mesh of steel), played an important part in the construction of the later skyscrapers, and this material also led to the introduction of more imaginative structural forms in buildings and to the development of prefabrication techniques. The use of large concrete members in bridges and other structures has been made possible by the technique of prestressing: By casting the concrete around stretched steel wires, allowing it to set, then relaxing the tension in the wires, it is possible to induce compressive stresses in the concrete that offset the tensile stresses imposed by the external loading, and in this way the members can be made stronger and lighter. The technique was particularly applicable in bridge building. The construction of large-span bridges received a setback, however, with the dramatic collapse of the Tacoma Narrows (Washington) Suspension Bridge in the United States in 1940, four months after it was completed. This led to a reassessment of wind effects on the loading of large suspension bridges and to significant improvements in subsequent designs. Use of massed concrete has produced spectacular high arch dams, in which the weight of water is transmitted in part to the abutments by the curve of the concrete wall; such dams need

The Hoover Dam was created using new methods that allowed engineers to build concrete gravity dams faster than ever in the 20th century.

not depend upon the sheer bulk of impervious material as in a conventional gravity or embankment dam.

TRANSPORTATION

Some of the outstanding achievements of the 20th century are provided by transportation history. In most fields there was a switch from steam power, supreme in the previous century, to internal combustion and electricity. Steam, however, retained its superiority in marine transport: the steam turbine provided power for a new generation of large ocean liners beginning with the *Mauretania*, developing 70,000 horsepower and a speed of 27 knots (27 nautical miles, or 50 km, per hour) in 1906 and continuing throughout the period, culminating in the *Queen Elizabeth*, launched in 1938 with about 200,000 horsepower and a speed of 28.5 knots. Even here, however, there was increasing competition from large diesel-powered motor vessels. Most smaller ships adopted this form of propulsion, and even the steamships accepted the convenience of oil-burning boilers in place of the cumbersome coal burners with their large bunkers.

On land, steam fought a long rearguard action, but the enormous popularity of the automobile deprived the railways of much of their passenger traffic and forced them to seek economies in conversion to diesel engines or electric traction, although these developments had not spread widely in Europe by the outbreak of World War II. Meanwhile, the automobile stimulated prodigious feats

Henry Ford's Model T was first produced using an assembly line in 1913, and within a decade annual production was up to nearly two million.

of production. Henry Ford led the way in the adoption of assembly-line mass production; his spectacularly successful Model T, the "Tin Lizzie," was manufactured in this way first in 1913, and by 1923 production had risen to nearly two million per year. Despite this and similar successes in other countries, the first half of the 20th century was not a period of great technological innovation in the motor-car, which retained the main design features given to it in the last decade of the 19th century. For all the refinements (for example, the self-starter) and countless varieties, the major fact of the automobile in this period was its quantity.

The airplane is entirely a product of the 20th century, unlike the automobile, to which its development was intimately related. This is not to say that experiments with flying machines had not taken place earlier. Throughout the 19th century, to go back no further, investigations into aerodynamic effects were carried out by inventors such as Sir George Cayley in England, leading to the successful glider flights of Otto Lilienthal and others. Several designers perceived that the internal-combustion engine promised to provide the light, compact power unit that was a prerequisite of powered flight, and on Dec. 17, 1903, Wilbur and Orville Wright in their *Flyer I* at Kill Devil Hills in North Carolina achieved sustained, controlled, powered flight, one of the great "firsts" in the history of technology. The *Flyer I* was a propeller-driven adaptation of the biplane gliders that the Wright brothers had built and learned to fly in the previous years. They had devised a system of control through elevator, rudder, and a wing-warping technique that served until the introduction of ailerons. Within a few years the brothers were flying with complete confidence, astonishing the European pioneers of flight when they took their airplane across the Atlantic to give demonstrations in 1908. Within a few months of this revelation, however, the European designers had assimilated the lesson and were pushing ahead the principles of aircraft construction. World War I gave a great impetus to this technological development, transforming small-scale scattered aircraft manufacture into a major industry in all the main belligerent countries and transforming the airplane itself from a fragile construction in wood and glue into a robust machine capable of startling aerobatic feats.

The end of the war brought a setback to this new industry, but the airplane had evolved sufficiently to reveal its potential as a medium of civil transport, and during the interwar years the establishment of transcontinental air routes provided a market for large, comfortable, and safe aircraft. By the outbreak of World War II, metal-framed-and-skinned aircraft had become general, and the cantilevered monoplane structure had replaced the biplane for most purposes. War again provided a powerful stimulus to aircraft designers; engine performance was especially improved, and the gas turbine received its first practical application. Other novel features of these years included the helicopter, deriving lift from its rotating wings, or rotors, and the German V-1 flying bomb, a pilotless aircraft.

The war also stimulated the use of gliders for the transport of troops, the use of parachutes for escape from aircraft and for attack by paratroops, and the use of gas-filled balloons for antiaircraft barrages. The balloon had been used for pioneer aeronautical experiments in the 19th century, but its practical uses had been hampered by the lack of control over its movements. The application of the internal-combustion engine to a rigid-frame balloon airship by Ferdinand von Zeppelin had temporarily made a weapon of war in 1915, although experience soon proved that it could not survive in competition with the airplane. The apparently promising prospects of the dirigible (that is, maneuverable) airship in civil transport between the wars were ended by a series of disasters, the worst of which was the destruction of the *Hindenburg* in New Jersey in 1937. Since then the airplane has been unchallenged in the field of air transport.

COMMUNICATIONS

The spectacular transport revolution of the 20th century was accompanied by a communications revolution quite as dramatic, although technologically springing from different roots. In part, well-established media of communication like printing participated in this revolution, although most of the significant changes—such as the typewriter, the Linotype, and the high-speed power-driven rotary press—were achievements of the 19th century. Photography was also a proved and familiar technique by the end of the 19th century, but cinematography was new and did not become generally available until after World War I, when it became enormously popular.

The real novelties in communications in the 20th century came in electronics. The scientific examination of the relationship between light waves and electromagnetic waves had already revealed the possibility of transmitting electromagnetic signals between widely separated points, and on Dec. 12, 1901, Guglielmo Marconi succeeded in transmitting

Guglielmo Marconi, c. 1908

the first wireless message across the Atlantic. Early equipment was crude, but within a few years striking progress was made in improving the means of transmitting and receiving coded messages. Particularly important was the development of the thermionic valve, a device for rectifying (that is, converting a high-frequency oscillating signal into a unidirectional current capable of registering as a sound) an electromagnetic wave. This was essentially a development from the carbon-filament electric lightbulb. In 1883 Edison had found that in these lamps a current flowed between the filament and a nearby test electrode, called the plate, if the electric potential of the plate was positive with respect to the filament. This current, called the Edison effect, was later identified as a stream of electrons radiated by the hot filament. In 1904 Sir John Ambrose Fleming of Britain discovered that by placing a metal cylinder around the filament in the bulb and by connecting the cylinder (the plate) to a third terminal, a current could be rectified so that it could be detected by a telephone receiver. Fleming's device was known as the diode, and two years later, in 1906, Lee De Forest of the United States made the significant improvement that became known as the triode by introducing a third electrode (the grid) between the filament and the plate. The outstanding feature of this refinement was its ability to amplify a signal. Its application made possible by the 1920s the widespread introduction of live-voice broadcasting in Europe and America, with a consequent boom in the production of radio receivers and other equipment.

This, however, was only one of the results derived from the application of the thermionic valve. The idea of harnessing the flow of electrons was applied in the electron microscope, radar (a detection device depending on the capacity of some radio waves to be reflected by solid objects), the electronic computer, and in the cathode-ray tube of the television set. The first experiments in the transmission of pictures had been greeted with ridicule. Working on his own in Britain, John Logie Baird in the 1920s demonstrated a mechanical scanner able to convert an image into a series of electronic impulses that could then be reassembled on a viewing screen as a pattern of light and shade. Baird's system, however, was rejected in favour of electronic scanning, developed in the United States by Philo Farnsworth and Vladimir Zworykin with the powerful backing of the Radio Corporation of America. Their equipment operated much more rapidly and gave a more satisfactory image. By the outbreak of World War II, television services were being introduced in several countries, although the war suspended their extension for a decade. The emergence of television as a universal medium of mass communication is therefore a phenomenon of the postwar years. But already by 1945 the cinema and the radio had demonstrated their power in communicating news, propaganda, commercial advertisements, and entertainment.

MILITARY TECHNOLOGY

It has been necessary to refer repeatedly to the effects of the two world wars in promoting all kinds of innovation. It should be observed also that technological innovations transformed the character of war itself. One weapon developed during World War II deserves a special mention. The principle of rocket propulsion was well known earlier, and its possibilities as a means of achieving speeds sufficient to escape from Earth's gravitational pull had been pointed out by such pioneers as the Russian Konstantin Tsiolkovsky and the American Robert H. Goddard. Goddard built experimental liquid-fueled rockets in 1926. Simultaneously, a group of German and Romanian pioneers was working along the same lines, and it was this team that was taken over by the German war effort in the 1930s and

A prototype, or test model, of the V-2 rocket is launched into space in 1942. This signaled the launch of the space age.

given the resources to develop a rocket capable of delivering a warhead hundreds of miles away. At the Peenemünde base on the island of Usedom in the Baltic, Wernher von Braun and his team created the V-2. Fully fueled, it weighed 14 tons; it was 40 feet (12 meters) long and was propelled by burning a mixture of alcohol and liquid oxygen. Reaching a height of more than 100 miles (160 kilometers), the V-2 marked the beginning of the space age, and members of its design team were instrumental in both the Soviet and U.S. space programs after the war.

Technology had a tremendous social impact in the period 1900 to 1945. The automobile and electric power, for instance, radically changed both the scale and the quality of 20th-century life, promoting a process of rapid urbanization and a virtual revolution in living through mass production of household goods and appliances. The rapid development of the airplane, the cinema, and radio made the world seem suddenly smaller and more accessible. In the years following 1945 the constructive and creative opportunities of modern technology would be exploited, although the process was not without its problems.

SPACE-AGE TECHNOLOGY

The years since World War II ended have been spent in the shadow of nuclear weapons, even though they have not been used in war since that time. These weapons underwent momentous development: the fission bombs of 1945 were superseded by the more powerful fusion bombs in 1950, and before 1960 rockets were shown capable of delivering these weapons at ranges of thousands of miles. This new military technology had an incalculable effect on international relations, for it contributed to the polarization of world power blocs while enforcing a caution, if not discipline, in the conduct of international affairs that was absent earlier in the 20th century.

The fact of nuclear power was by no means the only technological novelty of the post-1945 years. So striking indeed were the advances in engineering, chemical and medical technology, transport, and communications that some commentators wrote, somewhat misleadingly, of the "second Industrial Revolution" in describing the changes in these years. The rapid development of electronic engineering created a new world of computer technology, remote control, miniaturization, and instant communication. Even more expressive of the character of the period was the leap over the threshold of extraterrestrial exploration. The techniques of rocketry, first applied in weapons, were developed to provide launch vehicles for satellites and lunar and planetary probes and eventually, in 1969, to set the first men on the Moon and bring them home safely again. This astonishing achievement was stimulated in part by the international ideological rivalry already mentioned, as only the Soviet Union and the United States had both the resources and the will to support the huge expenditures required. It justifies the description of this period, however, as that of "space-age technology."

POWER

The great power innovation of this period was the harnessing of nuclear energy. The first atomic bombs represented only a comparatively crude form of nuclear fission, releasing the energy of the radioactive material immediately and explosively. But it was quickly appreciated that the energy released within a critical atomic pile, a mass of graphite absorbing the neutrons emitted by radioactive material inserted into it, could generate heat, which in turn could create steam to drive turbines and thus convert the nuclear energy into usable electricity. Atomic power stations were built on this principle in the advanced industrial world, and the system is still undergoing refinement, although so far atomic energy has not vindicated the high hopes placed in it as an economical source of electricity and presents formidable problems of waste disposal and maintenance. Nevertheless, it seems probable that the effort devoted to experiments on more direct ways of controlling nuclear fission will eventually produce results in power engineering.

Meanwhile, nuclear physics was probing the even more promising possibilities of harnessing the power of nuclear fusion, of creating the conditions in which simple atoms of hydrogen combine, with a vast release of energy, to form heavier atoms. This is the process that occurs in the stars, but so far it has only been created artificially by triggering off a fusion reaction with the intense heat generated momentarily by an

The first thermonuclear weapon (hydrogen bomb) was detonated at Enewetak atoll in the Marshall Islands, Nov. 1, 1952.

atomic fission explosion. This is the mechanism of the hydrogen bomb. So far scientists have devised no way of harnessing this process so that continuous controlled energy can be obtained from it, although researches into plasma physics, generating a point of intense heat within a stream of electrons imprisoned in a strong magnetic field, hold out some hopes that such means will be discovered in the not-too-distant future.

ALTERNATIVES TO FOSSIL FUELS

It may well become a matter of urgency that some means of extracting usable power from nuclear fusion be acquired. At the present rate of consumption, the world's resources of mineral fuels, and of the available radioactive materials used in the present nuclear power stations, will be exhausted within a period of perhaps a few decades. The most attractive alternative is thus a form of energy derived from a controlled fusion reaction that would use hydrogen from seawater, a virtually limitless source, and that would not create a significant problem of waste disposal. Other sources of energy that may provide alternatives to mineral fuels include various forms of solar cell, deriving power from the Sun by a

Solar panels use energy from sunlight to provide an alternative to fossil fuels.

chemical or physical reaction such as that of photosynthesis. Solar cells of this kind are already in regular use on satellites and space probes, where the flow of energy out from the Sun (the solar wind) can be harnessed without interference from the atmosphere or the rotation of the Earth.

MATERIALS

The space age spawned important new materials and uncovered new uses for old materials. For example, a vast range of applications have been found for plastics that have been manufactured in many different forms with widely varied characteristics. Glass fiber has been molded in rigid shapes to provide motor-car bodies and hulls for small ships. Carbon fiber has demonstrated remarkable properties

This drone, or unmanned aerial vehicle, was constructed from carbon fiber, which is an ideal material for blades that must withstand high temperatures.

that make it an alternative to metals for high-temperature turbine blades. Research on ceramics has produced materials resistant to high temperatures suitable for heat shields on spacecraft. The demand for iron and its alloys and for the nonferrous metals has remained high. The modern world has found extensive new uses for the latter: copper for electrical conductors, tin for protective plating of less-resistant metals, lead as a shield in nuclear power installations, and silver in photography. In most of these cases the development began before the 20th century, but the continuing increase in demand for these metals is affecting their prices in the world commodity markets.

DEVELOPMENTS IN COMPUTERS AND AUTOMATION

In the space age the most vital piece of equipment has been the computer, especially the electronic digital computer. The essence of this machine is the use of electronic devices to record electric impulses coded in the very simple binary system, using only two symbols. The Mark I digital computer was at work at Harvard University in 1944, and after World War II the possibility of using it for a wide range of applications was quickly realized. The early computers, however, were large and expensive machines, and their general application was delayed until the invention of the transistor revolutionized computer technology. The transistor is another of the key inventions of the space age. The product of research on the physics of solids, and particularly of those materials, such as germanium and silicon, known as semiconductors, the transistor was invented by John Bardeen, Walter H. Brattain, and William B. Shockley at Bell Telephone Laboratories in the United States in 1947. It was discovered that crystals of semiconductors, which have the capacity to conduct electricity in some conditions and not in others, could be made to perform the functions of a thermionic valve but in the form of a device that was much smaller, more reliable, and more versatile. The result has been the replacement of the cumbersome, fragile, and heat-producing vacuum tubes by the small and strong transistor in a wide range of electronic equipment. Most especially, this conversion has made possible the construction of much more powerful computers while making them more compact and less expensive.

The Harvard Mark I was more than 50 feet (15 m) long and contained some 750,000 parts. It was used to make calculations during World War II.

The potential for adaptation and utilization of the computer seems so great that many commentators have likened it to the human brain, and there is no doubt that human analogies have been important in its development. In Japan, where computer and other electronics technology made giant strides since the 1950s, fully computerized and automated factories were in operation by the mid-1970s, some of them employing complete workforces of robots in the manufacture of other robots. In the United States the chemical industry provides some of the most striking examples of fully automated, computer-controlled manufacture. The characteristics of continuous production lend themselves ideally to automatic control from a central computer monitoring the information fed back to it and making adjustments accordingly. Many large petrochemical plants producing materials for manufacturing industries are now run this way.

FOOD PRODUCTION

Food production has been subject to technological innovation such as accelerated freeze-drying and irradiation as methods of preservation, as well as the increasing mechanization of farming throughout the world. The widespread use of new pesticides and herbicides in some cases reached the point of abuse, causing worldwide concern. Despite such problems, farming was transformed in response to the demand for more food; scientific farming, with its careful breeding, controlled feeding, and mechanized handling, became commonplace. New food-producing techniques such as aquaculture and hydroponics, for farming the sea and seabed and for creating self-contained cycles of food production without soil, respectively, are being explored either to increase the world supply of food or to devise ways of

Hydroponic techniques allow plants to be grown without soil and may be a sustainable way to increase the food supply in needy areas.

sustaining closed communities such as may one day venture forth from the Earth on the adventure of interplanetary exploration.

CIVIL ENGINEERING

One industry that has not been deeply influenced by new control-engineering techniques is construction, in which the nature of the tasks involved makes dependence on a large labour force still essential, whether it be in constructing a skyscraper, a new highway, or a tunnel. Nevertheless, some important new techniques appeared since 1945, notably the use of heavy earth-moving and excavating machines such as the bulldozer and the tower crane. The use of prefabricated parts according to a predetermined system of construction became widespread. In the construction of housing units, often in large blocks of apartments or flats, such systems are particularly relevant because they make for standardization and economy in plumbing, heating, and kitchen equipment. The revolution in home equipment that began before World War II has continued apace since, with a proliferation of electrical equipment.

TRANSPORT AND COMMUNICATIONS

Many of these changes were facilitated by improvements in transport and communications. Transport developments have for the most part continued those well established in the early 20th century. The automobile proceeded in its phenomenal growth in popularity, causing radical changes in many of the patterns of life, although the basic design of the motorcar has remained unchanged. The airplane, benefiting from jet propulsion and a number of lesser technical advances, made spectacular gains at the expense of both the ocean liner and the railroad. However, the growing popularity of air transport brought problems of crowded airspace, noise, and airfield siting.

World War II helped bring about the shift to air transport: direct passenger flights across the Atlantic were initiated immediately after the war. The first generation of transatlantic airliners were the aircraft developed by war experience from the Douglas DC-3 and the pioneering types of the 1930s incorporating all-metal construction with stressed skin, wing flaps and slots, retractable landing gear, and other advances. The coming of the big jet-powered civil airliner in the 1950s kept pace with the rising demand for air services but accentuated the social problems of air transport. The solution to these problems may lie partly in the development of vertical takeoff and landing techniques, a concept successfully pioneered by a British military aircraft, the Hawker Siddeley Harrier. Longer-term solutions may be provided by the development of air-cushion vehicles derived from the Hovercraft, in use in the English Channel and elsewhere, and one of the outstanding technological innovations of the period since 1945. The central feature of this machine is a down-blast of air, which creates an air cushion on which the craft rides without direct contact with the sea or ground below it. The remarkable versatility of the air-cushion machine is beyond doubt, but it has proved difficult to find very many transportation needs that it can fulfill better than any craft already available. Despite these difficulties, it seems likely that this type of vehicle will have an important future. It should be remembered, however, that all the machines mentioned so far, automobiles, airplanes, and Hovercraft, use oil fuels, and it is possible that the exhaustion of these will turn attention increasingly to alternative sources of power and particularly to electric traction (electric railroads and autos), in which field there have been promising developments such as the linear-induction motor. Supersonic flight, for nearly 30 years an exclusive capability of military and research aircraft, became a commercial reality in 1975 with the Soviet Tu-144 cargo plane; the Concorde supersonic transport (SST), built jointly by the British and French governments, entered regular passenger service early in 1976.

In communications also, the dominant lines of development continue to be those that were established before or during World War II. In particular, the rapid growth of television services, with their immense influence as media of mass communication, was built on foundations laid in the 1920s and 1930s, while the universal adoption of radar on ships and airplanes followed the invention of a device to give early warning of aerial attack. But in certain features the development of communications in the space age has produced important innovations. First, the transistor, so significant for computers and control engineering, made a large contribution to communications technology. Second, the establishment of space satellites, considered to be a remote theoretical possibility in the 1940s, became part of the accepted technological scene in the 1960s, and these have played a dramatic part in telephone and television communication as well as in relaying meteorological pictures and data. Third, the development of magnetic tape as a means of recording sound and, more recently, vision provided a highly flexible and useful mode of communication. Fourth, new printing techniques were developed. In phototypesetting, a photographic image is substituted for the conventional metal type. In xerography, a dry copying process, an ink powder is attracted to the image to be copied by static electricity and then fused by heating. Fifth, new optical devices such as zoom lenses increased the power of cameras and prompted corresponding improvements in the quality of film available to the cinema and television. Sixth, new physical techniques, such as those that produced the laser (light amplification by stimulated emission of radiation), made available an immensely powerful means of communication over long distances, although these are still in their experimental stages. The laser also acquired significance as an important addition to surgical techniques and as an instrument of space weaponry. The seventh and final communications innovation is the use of electromagnetic waves other than light to explore the structure of the universe by means of the radio telescope and its derivative, the X-ray telescope. This technique was pioneered after World War II and has since become a vital instrument of satellite control and space research. Radio telescopes have also been directed toward the Sun's closest neighbors in

Radio telescopes are pointed toward objects close to the Sun in hopes of identifying signals that would suggest other intelligent life.

space in the hope of detecting electromagnetic signals from other intelligent species in the universe.

MILITARY TECHNOLOGY

Military technology in the space age has been concerned with the radical restructuring of strategy caused by the invention of nuclear weapons and the means of delivering them by intercontinental ballistic missiles. Apart from these major features and the elaborate electronic systems intended to give an early warning of missile attack, military reorganization has emphasized high maneuverability through helicopter transport and a variety of armed vehicles. Such forces were deployed in wars in Korea and Vietnam, the latter of which also saw the widespread use of napalm bombs and chemical defoliants to remove the cover provided by dense forests. World War II marked the end of the primacy of the heavily armoured battleship. Although the United States recommissioned several battleships in the 1980s, the aircraft carrier became the principal capital ship in the navies of the world. Emphasis now is placed on electronic detection and the support of nuclear-powered submarines equipped with missiles carrying nuclear warheads. The only major use of nuclear power since 1945, other than generating large-scale electric energy, has been the propulsion of ships, particularly missile-carrying submarines capable of cruising underwater for extended periods.

SPACE EXPLORATION

The rocket, which has played a crucial part in the revolution of military technology since the end of World War II, acquired a more constructive significance in the U.S. and Soviet space programs. The first spectacular step was Sputnik 1, a sphere with an instrument package weighing 184 pounds (83 kilograms), launched into space by the Soviets on Oct. 4, 1957, to become the first artificial satellite. The feat precipitated the so-called space race, in which achievements followed each other in rapid succession. They may be conveniently grouped in four chronological although overlapping stages.

The first stage emphasized increasing the thrust of rockets capable of putting satellites into orbit and on exploring the uses of satellites in communications, in weather observation, in monitoring military information, and in topographical and geological surveying.

The second stage was that of the manned space program. This began with the successful orbit of the Earth by the Soviet cosmonaut

Yury Gagarin on April 12, 1961, in the Vostok 1. This flight demonstrated mastery of the problems of weightlessness and of safe reentry into the Earth's atmosphere. A series of Soviet and U.S. spaceflights followed in which the techniques of space rendezvous and docking were acquired, flights up to a fortnight were achieved, and men "walked" in space outside their craft.

The third stage of space exploration was the lunar program, beginning with approaches to the Moon and going on through automatic surveys of its surface to manned landings. Again, the first achievement was Soviet: Luna 1, launched on Jan. 2, 1959, became the first artificial body to escape the gravitational field of the Earth, fly past the Moon, and enter an orbit around the Sun as an artificial planet. Luna 2 crashed on the Moon on Sept. 13, 1959; it was followed by Luna 3, launched on Oct. 4, 1959, which went around the Moon and sent back the first photographs of the side turned permanently away from the Earth. The first soft landing on the Moon was made by Luna 9 on Feb. 3, 1966; this craft carried cameras that transmitted the first photographs taken on the surface of the Moon. By this time excellent close-range photographs had been secured by the United States Rangers 7, 8, and 9, which crashed into the Moon in the second half of 1964 and the first part of 1965; and between 1966 and 1967 the series of five Lunar Orbiters photographed almost the entire surface of the Moon from a low orbit in a search for suitable landing places. The U.S. spacecraft Surveyor 1 made a soft landing on the Moon on June 2, 1966; this and following Surveyors acquired much useful information about the lunar surface. Meanwhile, the size and power of launching rockets climbed steadily, and by the late 1960s the enormous Saturn V rocket, standing 353 feet (108 meters) high and weighing 2,725 tons (2,472,000 kilograms) at liftoff, made possible the U.S. Apollo program, which climaxed on July 20, 1969, when Neil Armstrong and Edwin "Buzz" Aldrin clambered out of the Lunar Module of their Apollo 11 spacecraft onto the surface of the Moon. The manned lunar exploration thus begun continued with a widening range of experiments and achievements for a further five landings before the program was curtailed in 1972.

The fourth stage of space exploration looked out beyond the Earth and the Moon to the possibilities of planetary exploration. The U.S. space probe Mariner 2 was launched on Aug. 27, 1962, and passed by Venus the following December, relaying back information about that planet indicating that it was hotter and less hospitable than had been expected. These findings were confirmed by the Soviet Venera 3, which crash-landed on the planet on March 1, 1966, and by Venera 4, which made the first soft landing on Oct. 18, 1967. Later probes of the Venera series gathered further atmospheric and surficial data. The U.S. probe Pioneer Venus 1 orbited the planet for eight months in 1978, and in December of that year four landing probes conducted quantitative and qualitative analyses of the Venusian atmosphere. The surface temperature of approximately 900°F (482°C) reduced the functional life of such probes to little more than one hour.

Research on Mars was conducted primarily through the U.S. Mariner and Viking probe series. During the late 1960s, photographs from Mariner orbiters demonstrated a close visual resemblance between the surface of Mars and that of the Moon. In July and August 1976, Vikings 1 and 2, respectively, made successful landings on the planet; experiments designed to detect the presence or remains of organic material on the Martian surface met with mechanical difficulty, but results were generally interpreted as negative. Photographs taken during the early 1980s by the U.S. probes Voyagers 1 and 2 permitted unprecedented study of the atmospheres and satellites of Jupiter and Saturn and revealed a previously unknown configuration of rings around Jupiter, analogous to those of Saturn.

In the mid-1980s the attention of the U.S. space program was focused primarily upon the potentials of the reusable space shuttle vehicle for extensive orbital research. The U.S. space shuttle *Columbia* completed its first mission in April 1981 and made several successive flights. It was followed by the *Challenger*, which made its first mission in April 1983. Both vehicles were used to conduct myriad scientific experiments and to deploy satellites into orbit. The space program suffered a tremendous setback in 1986 when, at the outset of a *Challenger* mission, the shuttle exploded 73 seconds after liftoff, killing the crew of seven. The early 1990s saw mixed results for NASA. The $1.5 billion Hubble Space Telescope occasioned some disappointment when scientists discovered problems with its primary mirror after launch. A series of repairs and maintenance shuttle missions corrected the problem and kept the telescope operational into the 2010s. Interplanetary probes, to the delight of both professional and amateur stargazers, relayed beautiful, informative images of other planets.

NASA experienced another tragedy when the space shuttle *Columbia* disintegrated on reentry on February 1, 2003, killing its crew of seven. The United States ended its shuttle program in 2010 and turned to planning long-range, interplanetary missions. Reusable rockets designed by SpaceX began making low-earth orbits in 2010 and using unmanned spacecraft to deliver cargo to the International Space Station in 2012.

NASA launched two Mars rovers, Spirit and Opportunity, in 2003. They landed in 2004 and began exploring the terrain, relaying data to Earth that included evidence that water had once been present on Mars. Both rovers remained operational far

The Hubble Telescope sent back this photo of the Tarantula Nebula, a cloud of gas and dust, in 2012. NASA is working on the James Webb Space Telescope.

longer than expected, providing researchers with a wealth of new data.

In 2004, NASA and the European Space Agency joined forces to launch the Rosetta space probe to study comets. On August 6, 2014, NASA navigated a small landing module called Philae from Rosetta onto the surface of Comet 67P/Churyumov-Gerasimenko to gather data about its origins and composition.

NASA has continued to work on building a replacement for the Hubble Telescope. The James Webb Space Telescope is slated to launch in October 2018.

At the dawn of the space age it is possible to perceive only dimly its scope and possibilities. But it is relevant to observe that the history of technology has brought the world to a point in time at which humankind, equipped with unprecedented powers of self-destruction, stands on the threshold of extraterrestrial exploration.

CONTROVERSIES SURROUNDING SCIENCE AND TECHNOLOGY

The history of technology is longer than and distinct from the history of science. Technology is the systematic study of techniques for making and doing things; science is the systematic attempt to understand and interpret the world. While technology is concerned with the fabrication and use of artifacts, science is devoted to the more conceptual enterprise of understanding the environment, and it depends upon the comparatively sophisticated skills of literacy and numeracy. Such skills became available only with the emergence of the great world civilizations, so it is possible to say that science began with those civilizations, some 3,000 years BCE, whereas technology is as old as humanlike life. Science and technology developed as different and separate activities, the former being for several millennia a field of fairly abstruse speculation practiced by a class of aristocratic philosophers, while the latter remained a matter of essentially practical concern to craftsmen of many types. There were points of intersection, such as the use of mathematical concepts in building and irrigation work, but for the most part the functions of scientist and technologist (to use these modern terms retrospectively) remained distinct in the ancient cultures.

The situation began to change during the medieval period of development in the West (500–1500 CE), when both technical innovation and scientific understanding interacted with the stimuli of commercial expansion and a flourishing urban culture. The robust growth of technology in these centuries attracted the interest of educated men. Early in the 17th century the natural philosopher Francis Bacon recognized three great technological innovations—the magnetic compass, the printing press, and gunpowder—as the distinguishing achievements of modern man, and he advocated experimental science as a means of enlarging man's dominion over nature. By emphasizing a practical role for science in this way, Bacon implied a harmonization of science and technology, and he made his intention explicit by urging scientists to study the methods of craftsmen and urging craftsmen to learn more science. Bacon, with Descartes and other contemporaries, for the first time saw man becoming the master of nature, and a convergence between the traditional pursuits of science and technology was to be the way by which such mastery could be achieved.

Yet the wedding of science and technology proposed by Bacon was not soon consummated. Over the next 200 years, carpenters and mechanics—practical men of long standing—built iron bridges, steam engines, and textile machinery without much reference to scientific principles, while scientists—still amateurs—pursued their investigations in a haphazard manner. But the body of men, inspired by Baconian principles, who formed the Royal Society in London in 1660 represented a determined effort to direct scientific research toward useful ends, first by improving navigation and cartography, and ultimately by stimulating industrial innovation and the search for mineral resources. Similar bodies of scholars developed in other European countries, and by the 19th century scientists were moving toward a professionalism in which many of the goals were clearly the same as those of the technologists. Thus, Justus von Liebig of Germany, one of the fathers of organic chemistry and the first proponent of mineral fertilizer, provided the scientific impulse that led to the development of synthetic dyes, high explosives, artificial fibres, and plastics, and Michael Faraday, the brilliant British experimental scientist in the field of electromagnetism, prepared the ground that was exploited by Thomas A. Edison and many others.

EDISON'S ROLE

The role of Thomas A. Edison is particularly significant in the deepening relationship between science and technology because the prodigious trial-and-error process by which he selected the carbon filament for his electric lightbulb in 1879 resulted in the creation at Menlo Park, N.J., of what may be regarded as the world's first genuine industrial research laboratory. From this achievement the application of scientific principles to technology grew rapidly. It led easily to the engineering rationalism applied by Frederick W. Taylor to the organization of workers in mass production and to the time-and-motion studies of Frank and Lillian Gilbreth at the beginning of the 20th century. It provided a model

Thomas Alva Edison demonstrating his tinfoil phonograph, photograph by Mathew Brady, 1878.

that was applied rigorously by Henry Ford in his automobile assembly plant and that was followed by every modern mass-production process. It pointed the way to the development of systems engineering, operations research, simulation studies, mathematical modeling, and technological assessment in industrial processes. This was not just a one-way influence of science on technology because technology created new tools and machines with which the scientists were able to achieve an ever-increasing insight into the natural world. Taken together, these developments brought technology to its modern highly efficient level of performance.

CRITICISMS OF TECHNOLOGY

Judged entirely on its own traditional grounds of evaluation—that is, in terms of efficiency— the achievement of modern technology has been admirable. Voices from other fields, however, began to raise disturbing questions, grounded in other modes of evaluation, as technology became a dominant influence in society. In the mid-19th century the non-technologists were almost unanimously enchanted by the wonders of the new manmade environment growing up around them. London's Great Exhibition of 1851, with its arrays of machinery housed in the truly innovative Crystal Palace, seemed to be the culmination of Francis Bacon's prophetic forecast of man's increasing dominion over nature. The new technology seemed to fit the prevailing laissez-faire economics precisely and to guarantee the rapid realization of the Utilitarian philosophers' ideal of "the greatest good for the greatest number." Even Marx and Engels, espousing a radically different political orientation, welcomed technological progress because in their eyes it produced an imperative need for socialist ownership and control of industry. Similarly, early exponents

The transept of the Crystal Palace, designed by Sir Joseph Paxton, at the Great Exhibition of 1851, Hyde Park, London.

of science fiction such as Jules Verne and H.G. Wells explored with zest the future possibilities opened up to the optimistic imagination by modern technology, and the American utopian Edward Bellamy, in his novel *Looking Backward* (1888), envisioned a planned society in the year 2000 in which technology would play a conspicuously beneficial role.

Yet Ralph Waldo Emerson ominously warned, "Things are in the saddle and ride mankind." For the first time it began to seem as if "things"—the artifacts made by man in his campaign of conquest over nature—might get out of control and come to dominate him. Samuel Butler, in his satirical novel *Erewhon* (1872), drew the radical conclusion that all machines should be consigned to the scrap heap. And others such as William Morris, with his vision of a reversion to a craft society without modern technology, and Henry James, with his disturbing sensations of being overwhelmed in the presence of modern machinery, began to develop a profound moral critique of the apparent achievements of technologically dominated progress. Even H.G. Wells, despite all the ingenious and prophetic technological gadgetry of his earlier novels, lived to become disillusioned about the progressive character of Western civilization: His last book was titled *Mind at the End of Its Tether* (1945). In the film *Modern Times* (1936), Charlie Chaplin depicted the depersonalizing effect of the mass-production assembly line. Such images were given special potency by the international

J. Robert Oppenheimer

political and economic conditions of the 1930s, when the Western world was plunged in the Great Depression and seemed to have forfeited the chance to remold the world order shattered by World War I. In these conditions, technology suffered by association with the tarnished idea of inevitable progress.

Paradoxically, the escape from a decade of economic depression and the successful defense of Western democracy in World War II did not bring a return of confident notions about progress and faith in technology. The horrific potentialities of nuclear war were revealed in 1945, and the division of the world into hostile power blocs prevented any such euphoria and served to stimulate criticisms of technological aspirations even more searching than those that have already been mentioned. J. Robert Oppenheimer, who directed the design and assembly of the atomic bombs at Los Alamos, N.M., later opposed the decision to build the thermonuclear (fusion) bomb and described the accelerating pace of technological change with foreboding: "One thing that is new is the prevalence of newness, the changing scale and scope of change itself, so that the world alters as we walk in it, so that the years of man's life measure not some small growth or rearrangement or moderation of what he learned in childhood, but a great upheaval."

The theme of technological tyranny over individuality and traditional patterns of life was expressed by Jacques Ellul, of the University of Bordeaux, in his book *The Technological Society* (1964, first published as *La Technique* in 1954). Ellul asserted that technology had become so pervasive that man now lived in a milieu of technology rather than of nature. He characterized this new milieu as artificial, autonomous, self-determining, nihilistic (that is, not directed to ends, though proceeding by cause and effect), and, in fact, with means enjoying primacy over ends. Technology, Ellul held, had become so powerful and ubiquitous that other social phenomena such as politics and economics had become situated in it rather than influenced by it. The individual, in short, had come to be adapted to the technical milieu rather than the other way round.

While views such as those of Ellul have enjoyed a considerable vogue since World War II—and spawned a remarkable subculture of hippies and others who sought, in a variety of ways, to reject participation in technological society—it is appropriate to make two observations on them. The first is that these views are, in a sense, a luxury enjoyed only by advanced societies, which have benefited from modern technology. Few voices critical of technology can be heard in developing countries that are hungry for the advantages of greater productivity and the rising standards of living that have been seen to accrue to technological progress in the more fortunate developed countries.

The second observation about the spate of technological pessimism in the advanced countries is that it has not managed to slow the pace of technological advance, which seems, if anything, to have accelerated. The gap between the first powered flight and the first human steps on the Moon was only 66 years, and that between the disclosure of the fission of uranium and the detonation of the first atomic bomb was a mere six and a half years. The advance of the information revolution based on the electronic computer has been exceedingly swift, so that, despite the denials of the possibility by elderly and distinguished experts, the sombre spectre of sophisticated computers replicating higher human mental functions and even human individuality should not be relegated too hurriedly to the classification of science fantasy. The biotechnic stage of technological innovation is still in its infancy, and, if the recent rate of development is extrapolated forward, many seemingly impossible targets could be achieved in the next century. Not that this will be any consolation to the pessimists, as it only indicates the ineffectiveness to date of attempts to slow down technological progress.

THE TECHNOLOGICAL DILEMMA

Whatever the responses to modern technology, there can be no doubt that it presents contemporary society with a number of immediate problems that take the form of a traditional choice of evils, so that it is appropriate to regard them as constituting a "technological dilemma." This is the dilemma between, on the one hand, the overdependence of life in the advanced industrial countries on technology, and, on the other hand, the threat that technology will destroy the quality of life in modern society and even endanger society itself. Technology thus confronts Western civilization with the need to make a decision, or rather, a series of decisions, about how to use the enormous power available to society constructively rather than destructively. The need to control the development of technology, and so to resolve the dilemma, by regulating its application to creative social objectives, makes it ever more necessary to define these objectives while the problems presented by rapid technological growth can still be solved.

Nuclear Technology

Controlling nuclear technology, is primarily political. At its root is the anarchy of national self-government, for as long as the world remains divided into a multiplicity of nation-states, or even into power blocs, each committed to the defense of its own sovereign power to do what it chooses, nuclear weapons merely replace the older weapons by which such nation-states maintained their independence in the past. The availability of a nuclear armoury has emphasized the weaknesses of a world political system based upon sovereign nation-states. Here, as elsewhere, technology is a tool that can be used creatively or destructively. But the manner of its use depends entirely on human decisions, and in this matter of nuclear self-control the decisions are those of governments.

Ecological Balance

Another major problem area of modern technological society is that of preserving a healthy environmental balance. Though humans have been damaging the environment for centuries by overcutting trees and farming too intensively and though some protective measures, such as the establishment of national forests

Increasingly, efforts are being made to raise public awareness about the dangers of pollution and the importance of protecting the environment.

and wildlife sanctuaries, were taken decades ago, great increases in population and in the intensity of industrialization are promoting a worldwide ecological crisis. Great public concern about pollution in the advanced nations is both overdue and welcome. Once more, however, it needs to be said that the fault for this waste-making abuse of technology lies with man himself rather than with the tools he uses. For all his intelligence, man in communities behaves with a lack of respect for the environment that is both shortsighted and potentially suicidal.

TECHNOLOGY SHAPING SOCIETY

M uch of the 19th-century optimism about the progress of technology has dispersed. And an increasing awareness of the technological dilemma confronting the world makes it possible to offer a realistic assessment of the role of technology in shaping society today.

INTERACTIONS BETWEEN SOCIETY AND TECHNOLOGY

The relationship between technology and society is a complex one. Any technological stimulus can trigger a variety of social responses, depending on such unpredictable variables as differences between human personalities; similarly, no specific social situation can be relied upon to produce a determinable

For all the excitement over technology in the 19th century, today there is a more skeptical view of how it shapes our society.

technological response. Any "theory of invention," therefore, must remain extremely tentative, and any notion of a "philosophy" of the history of technology must allow for a wide range of possible interpretations. A major lesson of the history of technology, indeed, is that it has no precise predictive value. It is frequently possible to see in retrospect when one particular artifact or process had reached obsolescence while another promised to be a highly successful innovation, but at the time such historical hindsight is not available and the course of events is indeterminable. In short, the complexity of human society is never capable of resolution into a simple identification of causes and effects driving historical development in one direction rather than another, and any attempt to identify technology as an agent of such a process is unacceptable.

THE POWER AND LIMITS OF TECHNOLOGY

The definition of technology as the systematic study of techniques for making and doing things establishes technology as a social phenomenon and thus as one that cannot possess complete autonomy, unaffected by the society in which it exists.

The 2014 Light + Building trade fair in Germany featured the theme, "Explore Technology for Life—the best energy is the energy that is not consumed."

(continued on the next page)

(continued from the previous page)

It is necessary to make what may seem to be such an obvious statement because so much autonomy has been ascribed to technology, and the element of despair in interpretations like that of Jacques Ellul is derived from an exaggerated view of the power of technology to determine its own course apart from any form of social control. Admittedly, once a technological development, such as the introduction of electricity for domestic lighting, is firmly established, it is difficult to stop it before the process is complete. The assembly of resources and the arousal of expectations both create a certain technological momentum that tends to prevent the process from being arrested or deflected. Nevertheless, the decisions about whether to go ahead with a project or to abandon it are undeniably human, and it is a mistake to represent technology as a monster or a juggernaut threatening human existence. In itself, technology is neutral and passive: In the phrase of Lynn White, Jr., "Technology opens doors; it does not compel man to enter." Or, in the words of the traditional adage, it is a poor craftsman who blames his tools, and so, just as it was naive for 19th-century optimists to imagine that technology could bring paradise on Earth, it seems equally simplistic for pessimists today to make technology itself a scapegoat for human shortcomings.

TECHNOLOGY AND EDUCATION

In the early millennia of human existence, a craft was acquired in a lengthy and laborious manner by serving with a master who gradually trained the initiate in the arcane mysteries of the skill. Such instruction, set in a matrix of oral tradition and practical experience, was frequently more closely related to religious ritual than to the application of rational scientific principles. Thus, the artisan in ceramics or sword making protected the skill while ensuring that it would be perpetuated. Craft training was institutionalized in Western civilization in the form of apprenticeship, which has survived as a framework for instruction in technical skills. Increasingly, however, instruction in new techniques requires

A Navajo weaver works outdoors in Arizona. Traditional weaving methods and other hands-on skills are in declining demand in modern times.

access both to general theoretical knowledge and to realms of practical experience that, on account of their novelty, were not available through traditional apprenticeship. Thus, the requirement for a significant proportion of academic instruction has become an important feature of most aspects of modern technology. This accelerated the convergence between science and technology in the 19th and 20th centuries and created a complex system of educational awards representing the level of accomplishment from simple instruction in schools to advanced research in universities. French and German academies led in the provision of such theoretical instruction, while Britain lagged somewhat in the 19th century, owing to its long and highly successful tradition of apprenticeship in engineering and related skills. But by the 20th century all the advanced industrial countries, including newcomers like Japan, had recognized the crucial role of a theoretical technological education in achieving commercial and industrial competence.

The recognition of the importance of technological education, however, has never been complete in Western civilization, and the continued coexistence of other traditions has caused problems of assimilation and adjustment. The British author C.P. Snow drew attention to one of the most persistent problems in his perceptive essay *The Two Cultures* (1959), in which he identified the dichotomy between scientists and technologists on the one hand and humanists and artists on the

Sir C.P. Snow

other as one between those who did understand the second law of thermodynamics and those who did not, causing a sharp disjunction of comprehension and sympathy. Arthur Koestler put the same point in another way by observing that the traditionally humanities-educated Westerner is reluctant to admit that a work of art is beyond comprehension but will cheerfully confess to not understanding how a radio or heating system works. Koestler

Black-box technology is only an arm's length away in many of the most modern automobiles.

characterized such a modern individual as an "urban barbarian," isolated from a technological environment that he or she possesses without understanding. Yet the growing prevalence of "black-box" technology, in which only the rarefied expert is able to understand the enormously complex operations that go on inside the electronic equipment, makes it more and more difficult to avoid becoming such a barbarian. The most helpful development would seem to be not so much seeking to master the expertise of others in our increasingly specialized society as encouraging those disciplines that provide bridges between the two cultures, and here there is a valuable role for the history of technology.

THE QUALITY OF LIFE

Concern with the quality of life can be identified in the relationship between technology and society. There can be little doubt that technology has brought a higher standard of living to people in advanced countries, just as it has enabled a rapidly rising population to subsist in the developing countries. It is the prospect of rising living standards that makes the acquisition of technical competence so attractive to these countries. But however desirable the possession of a comfortable

sufficiency of material goods, and the possibility of leisure for recreative purposes, the
quality of a full life in any human society has
other even more important prerequisites, such
as the possession of freedom in a law-abiding
community and of equality before the law.
These are the traditional qualities of democratic societies, and it has to be asked whether
technology is an asset or a liability in acquiring
them. Certainly, highly illiberal regimes have
used technological devices to suppress individual freedom and to secure obedience to the
state: the nightmare vision of George Orwell's
Nineteen Eighty-four (1949), with its telescreens
and sophisticated torture, has provided liter-
ary demonstration of this reality, should one
be needed. But the fact that high technological competence requires, as has been shown,
a high level of educational achievement by
a significant proportion of the community
holds out the hope that a society that is well
educated will not long endure constraints
on individual freedom and initiative that are
not self-justifying. In other words, the high
degree of correlation between technological success and educational accomplishment
suggests a fundamental democratic bias
about modern technology. It may take time
to become effective, but, given sufficient
time without a major political or social

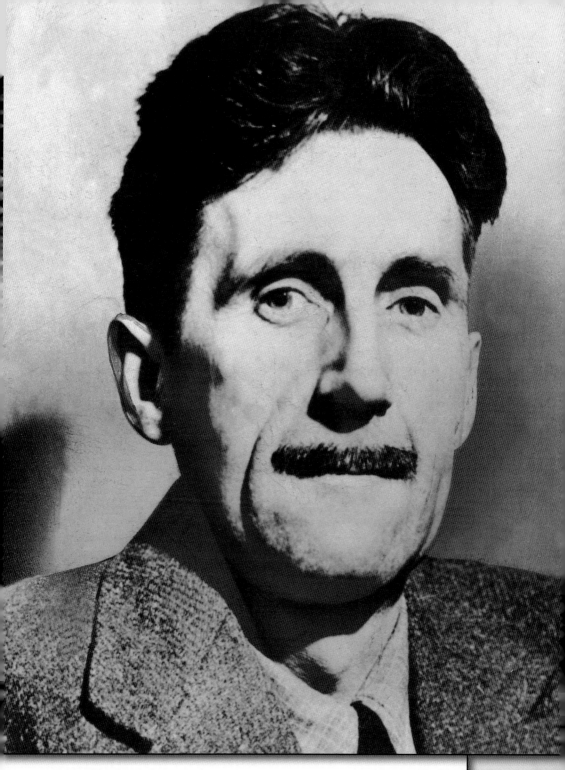

George Orwell

disruption and a consequent resurgence of national assertiveness and human selfishness, there are sound reasons for hoping that technology will bring the people of the world into a closer and more creative community.

Such, at least, must be the hope of anybody who takes a long view of the history of technology as one of the most formative and persistently creative themes in the development of humankind from the Paleolithic cave dwellers of antiquity to the dawn of the space age. Above all other perceptions of technology, the threshold of space exploration on which humankind stands provides the most dynamic and hopeful portent of human potentialities. Even while the threat of technological self-destruction remains ominous and the problems of population control and ecological imbalance cry out for satisfactory solutions, man has found a clue of his own future in terms of a quest to explore and colonize the depths of an infinitely fascinating universe. As yet, only a few visionaries have appreciated the richness of this possibility, and their projections are too easily dismissed as nothing more than imaginative science fiction. But in the long run, if there is to be a long run for our uniquely technological but willful species, the future depends upon the ability to acquire such a cosmic perspective, so it is important to recognize this now and to begin the arduous mental and physical preparations accordingly. The words of Arthur C. Clarke, one of the most perceptive of contemporary seers, in his *Profiles of the Future* (1962), are worth recalling in this context. Thinking ahead to

Arthur C. Clarke

the countless aeons that could stem from the remarkable human achievement summarized in the history of technology, he surmised that the all-knowing beings who may evolve from these humble beginnings may still regard our own era with wistfulness: "But for all that, they may envy us, basking in the bright after-glow of Creation; for we knew the Universe when it was young."

The technological breakthroughs that began in the early 20th century have provided humanity with numerous benefits and opportunities. Advances have led to improved health care for many, better farming techniques, faster travel, and instant communication. Improved materials, automated manufacturing techniques, and global shipping

Technology, for all its advances, still has not solved all the world's problems, such as how to handle pollution and preserve the environment.

networks have lowered the cost of goods and made many modern conveniences available to people who might not have been able to afford them at an earlier time. The daily lives of people in distant places are now much more closely connected than ever before through the Internet. Technology has taken people to the Moon, and scientists are striving to find a way to reach deeper into the solar system.

At the same time, technology has not solved many of the world's problems. Many people still do not have enough food to eat or access to clean drinking water. Pollution and environmental degradation are just two of the consequences of technology's rapid evolution. Global warming has been linked to carbon emissions from sources such as factories and automobiles. Researchers continue to look for ways to slow this process, while inventors and innovators look for more ways to improve the world through technology.

aeon An immeasurably or indefinitely long period of time.

aero-engine An engine designed to power an aircraft.

autonomy The power or right of self-government.

biotechnic Concerned with the adaptation of technology to the betterment of human life.

biplane An airplane with two main supporting surfaces usually placed one above the other.

cantilever A projecting beam or member supported at only one end.

defoliant A chemical spray or dust applied to crop plants (as cotton that is to be harvested with a stripper) to cause the leaves to drop off prematurely.

diesel engine An internal-combustion engine in which air is compressed to a temperature sufficiently high to ignite fuel injected directly into the cylinder where the combustion and expansion actuate a piston.

diode An electronic device with two electrodes that is used especially for changing alternating current into direct current.

dirigible Capable of being steered.

electrode A conductor (as a metal or carbon) used to make electrical contact with a part of an electrical circuit that is not metallic.

filament Thin wire in a light bulb that glows when electricity passes through it.

fission The splitting of an atomic nucleus resulting in the release of large amounts of energy.

hydroponics The growing of plants in nutrient solutions.

hyperbole Language that describes something as better or worse than it really is.

Industrial Revolution An economic revolution (as in England beginning in about 1760) characterized by a marked acceleration in the output of industrial goods correlative with the introduction of power-driven machinery into industry and consequent decline of handwork and domestic production.

internal-combustion engine A heat engine in which the combustion that generates the heat takes place inside the engine proper instead of in a furnace.

Iron Age The period of human culture characterized by the smelting of iron and its almost universal use in industry beginning about 1000 BCE in southern Europe and somewhat earlier in western Asia and Egypt.

jet propulsion The forward motion of a body by means of a jet of fluid (as in the motion given to an inflated toy balloon when the compressed air is allowed to escape through the neck or the motion given to a rocket by the rearward discharge of a high-speed stream of hot gases produced by the rocket fuel).

juggernaut Something (such as a force, campaign, or movement) that is extremely large and powerful and cannot be stopped.

linear-induction motor A motor that used high-powered magnets to launch coasters like a slingshot, enabling them, for example, to reach speeds of 70 miles (112.5 km) per hour in under four seconds.

Linotype Used for a typesetting machine that produces each line of type in the form of a solid metal slug.

microchip A group of tiny electronic circuits that work together on a very small piece of hard material (such as silicon).

oscillating Swinging backward and forward like a pendulum.

piston A sliding piece moved by or moving against fluid pressure that usually consists of a short cylindrical body fitting within a cylindrical chamber or vessel along which it moves back and forth.

plasma physics A branch of physics that deals with magnetohydrodynamic phenomena, of or relating to phenomena arising from the motion of electrically conducting fluids in the presence of electric and magnetic fields.

rover Unmanned, wheeled robotic roving vehicle that investigate the surface of other planets, such as the Curiosity rover.

thermionic valve A two-electrode vacuum tube.

truss A rigid framework of beams, bars, or rods.

turbine an engine whose central driving shaft is fitted with a series of blades spun around by the pressure of a fluid (as water, steam, or air).

Canadian Science and Technology Historical Association (CSTHA)
Box 8502, Stn. T,
Ottawa, ON K1G 3H9
Canada
Website: http://cstha-ahstc.ca
The Canadian Science and Technology Historical Association (CSTHA) was founded in 1980 "and is a national society devoted to the study of the history of Canadian science and technology. Our primary mission is to make our scientific and technical history better known and to make this subject an important element in Canadian historiography."

European Association for the Study of Science and Technology (EASST)
EASST Office
Bodemsweg 2
6225 ND Maastricht
The Netherlands
Website: http://easst.net
Established in 1981, the European Association for the Study of Science and Technology is a nonprofit organization that "represents academics and researchers in the fields of science and technology studies, the social analysis of innovation and related areas of

knowledge. It brings together a variety of disciplines and many of its members have qualifications in both natural science/engineering and social sciences."

Foundation for the History of Technology (SHT)
FAO Secretariat
c/o Eindhoven University of Technology
Faculty of Industrial Engineering & Innovation Sciences
IPO-building, Room 2.31
P.O. Box 513
5600 MB Eindhoven
The Netherlands
Website: http://www.histech.nl/www/en/home
Established in 1988, the Foundation for the History of Technology (SHT) advocates the enhanced perception of technology's importance in the modern world's history.

International Committee for the History of Technology (ICOHTEC)
c/o Institute for the History of Science
Polish Academy of Sciences
ul. Nowy Swiat 72, pok. 9
00-330 Warsaw
POLAND
Website: www.icohtec.org
Founded in Paris in 1968, the International

Committee for the History of Technology (ICOHTEC) strives to foster relationships among different disciplines for international cooperation in the study of technology. It also supports the study, research, and documentation of the rich history of technology.

Museum of Science and Industry
5700 S Lake Shore Drive
Chicago, IL 60637
(773) 684-1414
Website: http://www.msichicago.org
The Museum of Science and Industry, Chicago (MSI) is "the largest science museum in the Western Hemisphere, is home to more than 35,000 artifacts and more than 400,000 square feet of hands-on experiences designed to spark scientific inquiry and creativity."

Society for the History of Technology (SHOT)
Department of History
310 Thach Hall
Auburn University, AL 36849-5207
(334) 844-6770
Website: http://www.historyoftechnology.org
Founded in 1958, SHOT's focus is on "historical study of technology and its relations with politics, economics, labor, business, the environment, public policy, science, and the

arts." This international society has members from more than 35 countries.

WEBSITES

Because of the changing nature of Internet links, Rosen Publishing has developed an online list of websites related to the subject of this book. This site is updated regularly. Please use this link to access the list:
http://www.rosenlinks.com/TECH/Mod

Creeley, Robert. *Breakthroughs in Telephone Technology*: From Bell to Smartphones. New York, NY: Britannica Educational Publishing, 2011.

Evans, Lyndon, editor. *The Large Hadron Collider*: A Marvel of Technology. Boca Raton, FL: EFPL Press, 2014.

Ferris, Julie, and Mike Goldsmith. *Ideas that Changed the World*. New York, NY: DK Publishing, 2013.

Ganchy, Sally. *Islam And Science, Medicine, And Technology*. New York, NY: Rosen Publishing, 2009.

McCollum, Sean. *The Fascinating, Fantastic Unusual History of Robots (Unusual Histories)*. Mankato, MN: Capstone Press, 2012.

McFadzean, Lesley. *Technology and Treatments*. New York, NY: Rosen Publishing, 2012.

McPherson, Stephanie Sammartino. *War of the Currents: Thomas Edison vs. Nikola Tesla*. Minneapolis, MN: Twenty-First Century Books, 2013.

Shea, Therese. *Gamification: Using Gaming Technology For Achieving Goals*. New York, NY: Rosen Publishing, 2013.

Sheinkin, Steve. *Bomb: The Race to Build—and Steal—the World's Most Dangerous Weapon*. New York, NY: Roaring Brook Press, 2012.

Smith, Terry L. *Modern Genetic Science: New*

Technology, New Decisions. New York, NY: Rosen Publishing, 2009.

Sterngass, Jon. *Controversy!: Reproductive Technology.* New York, NY: Marshall Cavendish Benchmark, 2012.

Woolf, Alex. *The Impact of Technology in History and Archaeology.* Chicago, IL: Heinemann Raintree, 2015.